The Workers Opposition in the Russian Communist Party

The Fight for Workers Democracy in the Soviet Union

by Alexandra Kollontai

Red and Black Publishers, St Petersburg, Florida

Published in 1921 by the Industrial Workers of the World

Library of Congress Cataloging-in-Publication Data

Kollontai, A. (Aleksandra), 1872-1952.
   The workers opposition in the Russian Communist Party : the fight for workers democracy in the Soviet Union / by Alexandra Kollontai.
      p. cm.
   Originally published: Chicago : Industrial Workers of the World, 1921.
   ISBN 978-1-934941-70-6
1. Labor unions--Soviet Union. I. Title.
   JN6598.K7K541413 2009
   322'.2094709042--dc22

                                            2009016085

Red and Black Publishers, PO Box 7542, St Petersburg, Florida, 33734
Contact us at: info@RedandBlackPublishers.com
Printed and manufactured in the United States of America

Contents

Preface

The history of the Workers' Opposition has been largely forgotten, both in the West and in the former Soviet Union. This is unfortunate, since it is the history of a faction within the Russian Communist Party itself which, during the very time that the Russian Revolution was falling into the centralization of political and economic power that would shortly lead to Stalin's dictatorship, stood up to defend socialism, democracy, workers' control, the rights of union workers, and economic justice. Sadly, their struggle was in vain—the bureaucratic Party concentrated all power in its hands, and Stalin soon assumed sole power and crushed the people of the Soviet Union under one of the most brutal regimes of the 20th century. Many of the members of the Workers' Opposition died in Stalin's jails.

The ideas that were advocated by the Workers' Opposition had deep roots in the history of the Russian Revolution. In January 1905, a large peaceful demonstration was led by an Orthodox Priest, George Gapon, to the Czar's Winter Palace, with a petition asking for freedom and democracy. They were fired on by Czarist troops, and "Bloody Sunday" became the rallying cry for revolution. Over the next few months, demonstrations and protests took place across Russia, and some three million workers walked out on strike.

In May, in the city of Ivanovno-Voznesensk, some 70,000 striking textile workers elected a strike committee, known as a Soviet (from the Russian word for "council"). Soon, workers, peasants and soldiers in nearly every sizable city in Russia elected their own local Soviets, and these began taking on political tasks and functioning more and more as quasi-governmental powers, in many cases organizing their own armed militias and passing and enforcing their own laws and regulations. In the larger industrial cities, like Moscow and St Petersburg, the Soviets became strong enough to directly challenge the authority of the Czarist government (in St Petersburg, the Soviet declared on its own authority an end to the Czar's censorship, and banned the city's printers from publishing anything that had been submitted to the Czar's censors), and plans were being made for each municipal and regional Soviet to send delegates to a national Soviet to form a provisional national government. By September 1905, the Soviets had become powerful enough to call out a nationwide general strike that completely paralyzed the entire country. Within a month, the Czar was forced to give in, and signed the October Manifesto granting a constitution and an elected legislature known as the Duma.

With that concession, the revolt died down, and the Czarist police moved quickly to crush the remaining Soviets. All the leaders of the St Petersburg Soviet were arrested (including a young radical named Leon Trotsky). In Moscow, the Soviet called on its workers to go out on strike again and throw up barricades in protest, but the rebellion was easily beaten by Czarist troops. By December 1905, the Soviets were gone and the revolt had ended.

In March 1917, though, the same basic process was repeated. Wearied by the poverty and hunger brought about by the First World War, workers spontaneously went out on strike all over

Russia. As the bread riots and strikes became more political in character, local Soviets were again elected. The most important of these was the Petrograd Soviet (the city of St Petersburg had been renamed to Petrograd after the war had started), which was elected in the middle of March. Other Soviets appeared in hundreds of other cities, and the All-Russian Central Executive Committee was formed in Petrograd to coordinate all of the local Soviets. The political slogan adopted by the revolution was "All power to the Soviets!" When the Czar abdicated and a Provisional Government formed by the Duma took power, the Soviets remained intact, in many areas exercising more authority than the new Provisional Government did.

At the time the Czarist government fell, the Soviets were dominated by representatives of the peasant-based Social Revolutionary Party and the Menshevik faction of the leftist Russian Social Democratic Party. Over the next several months, however, the Bolshevik faction of the Social Democrats, led by Lenin, gained control of the major Soviets. When Kerensky's Provisional Government floundered over economic troubles and its decision to continue the unpopular participation of Russia in the First World War, the Bolsheviks organized a successful bloodless coup in November 1917, transferring power from the Provisional Government to the Bolshevik-dominated Soviets. For the next four years, Russia was wracked by civil war, as the Bolsheviks were opposed by a loose collection of former Czarists, conservative peasants, foreign troops (including Americans), and non-Bolshevik socialists and anarchists.

By 1921, the Russian Civil War was over, and the Bolsheviks stood as the only remaining power in Russia. In the 1918 Constitution, political power was, theoretically, centered in the local democratically-elected Soviets. The local Soviets elected representatives to the national Council of People's Commissars, which in turn elected a Chairman as head of state. The Council also elected the heads of the various Commissariats, or governmental departments, which had responsibility for various areas of government.

Very quickly, however, the Soviet-based government became subordinated to the ruling Communist Party. All of the real political and economic power lay within the Communist Party's Political Bureau (Politburo), which was elected by the Party Central Committee. The Soviet government quickly became a rubber stamp for decisions made by the Politburo.

In February 1921, the sailors at the Kronstadt Fortress mutinied in an attempt to overthrow the Communist Party and re-institute direct elected worker control through the Soviet government. The rebellion was crushed by Red Army troops.

The Workers' Opposition was a faction within the Communist Party that advocated the same return to democratic Soviet government, as well as direct worker control of industries through elected managements set up by the trade unions.

Most of the members of the Workers' Opposition were trade union officials. The most prominent spokesperson for the Workers' Opposition was Alexander Shlyapnikov, who was Chairman of the Russian Metalworkers Union. He was joined by fellow Metalworkers Union officials Sergei Medvedev and Mikhail Vladimirov, and by Textile Workers Union official Ivan Kutuzov, Miner's Union Chairman Alexei Kiselev, Yuri Lutovinov of the All-Russian Council of Trade Unions, Mikhail Chelyshev of the Party Control Commission, Kiril Orlov of the Council of Military Industry, and others.

Although not a trade unionist, one of the most outspoken supporters of the Workers' Opposition was Alexandra Kollontai.

"The Workers' Opposition in the Russian Communist Party" was written by Kollantai as a paper for the 10th Congress of the Communist Party, held in 1921. Although the Congress elected Shlyapnikov to the Central Committee and adopted some of the positions advocated by the Workers' Opposition, including a removal of some party members and a pledge to divert more resources to improving workers' lives, it condemned the Workers' Opposition itself for "factionalism", and suppressed all its writings. At the 11th Party Congress in 1922, Shlyapnikov, Kollantai and Medvedev were almost expelled from the Communist Party after circulating a paper criticizing the suppression of dissent in the Party and condemning the domination of the trade unions by Party functionaries.

After this, most of the former Oppositionists were forced to temper their criticism. Kollantai was appointed Ambassador to Norway, and later to Sweden and Mexico. She was never again able to exercise any influence on Party policy. Her virtual exile abroad probably saved her life.

Stalin was elected General Secretary of the Politburo in 1922. After Lenin died in 1924, Stalin used his control of the Politburo to become the sole power in the Communist Party, and ruled Russia as a virtual autocrat. The Soviet Union revealed itself as an institution of bureaucratic state capitalism, in which worker control was crushed, independent labor unions were actively destroyed, and the only acceptable role for workers was to shut up, get back to work, and produce wealth for the benefit of the privileged elite.

In 1926, members of the now-banned Workers' Opposition tried to prevent Stalin's grab for power, but failed. In a series of purges, Stalin removed all the "disloyal elements" from the Party and executed them. Shlyapnikov and Medvedev were both shot in September 1937. The rest died in gulag prisons. Kollontai, who no longer had any ability to influence events in the Soviet Union, was the only survivor. She died of natural causes in 1952.

Even in death, however, the Workers' Oppositionists had the final say. When the Leninist state capitalism finally collapsed in 1989, it was striking miners in the Ukraine, and the appearance of the independent labor union Solidarity in Poland, that provoked the USSR's downfall.

Editor

Red and Black Publishers

2009

Introduction

The principal object in translating and publishing this book is to show the workers in America a revolutionary political party in operation, and to demonstrate its inevitable tendency towards bureaucracy with a consequent isolation from the masses. A complete survey or even a small part of the evils abounding in a political centralization of production and distribution is of course beyond the scope of this small book and too, it is obvious that the complaint expressed here could not tread outside of party lines.

The book was only intended originally for the delegates of the Tenth Congress of the Russian Communist Party, and, anticipating criticism for publishing in America what was not intended for the world at large, we justify ourselves on the ground that of a party having perhaps the destiny and welfare of the millions of Russia in their hands is as much the business of revolutionary workers in America as anywhere else. Yes, even Russian workers.

The Russian Revolution as a spontaneous movement of the masses is not the property of any certain group or party. All humanity is bound up in such an event and therefore no one can be expected to recognize certain circles beyond which a knowledge of such vital questions cannot go.

The failure of the Bolshevik party to solve the social problem and the failure of the author of this book to prove that it could have been solved by the same political party if they only had adopted the tactics suggested by the "Opposition", these two facts taken together should, in our opinion, be sufficient to remove for a long time to come the notion that a few leaders can emancipate the workers, from their desks in government buildings.

Kollontai has succeeded in convincing us that Lenin, Trotsky and Zinoviev together with other front rank Bolsheviks were wrong all the time in trying to solve the social problem from the top downward. She has strengthened the belief that it must take place from the bottom upward, but she has failed to show any logical justification for a political party directing such a movement.

The translation of this book from Russian to English presented many difficulties, chief of which was the necessity of remodeling many parts into readable English. The original in Russian was written in haste, with barely time to have it printed for the Tenth Congress of the Russian Communist Party, and this made it impossible for a better and more studious attention to the details of construction. Therefore the English translation bears many sentences and paragraphs that are not exact translations, but retain the sense of the original copy. One other thing that must be noted in connection with the book is the intimate manner the writer assumes. This is of course because her intended auditors were familiar with the situation with which she was dealing and therefore she was excluded from the necessity of going very deep in her discussions. But in spite of all this, it is obvious that the "Infantile Sickness of Leftism" is a disease that is completely overshadowed by the organic weakness of political centers.

This book is now out of print in Russia and together with the "Workers' Opposition" as a movement was officially declared by the Tenth Congress of the Russian Party to be, "incompatible with the present policy of the Communist Party", and as this can mean nothing else than that the stamp of illegality has been placed on the movement, it must now operate outside of party influences. What will be the future of the "Opposition" principles in Russia one can only guess, but it is certain that the struggle of the workers to control the industries themselves will be carried on in Russia in spite of all legal hindrances.

Industrial Workers Of The World

1921

The Workers' Opposition in the Russian Communist Party

What Is The Workers' Opposition?

What is the "Workers' Opposition"? Is it necessary on behalf of our party and the world workers' revolution to welcome its existence, or is it just the contrary, that the phenomenon is a harmful one, dangerous "politically", as comrade Trotsky just recently stated in one of his speeches on the trade union question?

In order to answer these questions which are agitating and perturbing many of our fellow workers, it is necessary to make clear:

1. Who enters into the Workers' Opposition, and how has it originated?

2. Where is the root of the controversy between the leading comrades of our party centers and the Workers' Opposition?

It is very significant—and to this must be drawn the attention of our central bodies—that the Workers' Opposition is composed of the most advanced part of our class-organized proletarian communists. The Opposition consists almost exclusively of members of the trade unions, and this fact is attested by the signatures of those who side with the opposition under the theses on the role of industrial unions. Who are these members of the trade unions? Workers—that part of the advanced guard of the Russian proletariat which has borne on its shoulders all the difficulties of the revolutionary struggle, and did not dissolve itself into the Soviet institutions by losing contact with the laboring masses, but on the contrary, remained closely connected with them.

To remain a member in the union, to preserve the close vital contact with one's union, and hence, with the workers of one's industry, through all these stormy years, when the center of social and political life has been shifted away from the unions, is not at all an easy and simple task. Foamy waves of the revolution have caught and carried far away from the unions the best, the strongest and the most active elements of the industrial proletariat, throwing one to the military front, another into the Soviet institutions, and seating a third by desks covered with green office table cloth and heaps of office papers, books, estimates, and projects.

The unions have been depopulated. And only workers imbued with the strongest proletarian spirit, the real blossom of the rising revolutionary class, remained immune to the dissipating influence of authority, of petty ambition and high positions in Soviet bureaucracy. They still stay spiritually welded together with the masses of the workers: that lowest stratum of society from whom they themselves came, an organic connection which could not be severed even by the highest Soviet positions.

As soon as the intensity of the struggle on the fronts diminished, and the pendulum of life swung on the side of economic reconstruction, these representative, inveterate proletarians in spirit, the most luminous and staunchest of their own class, rapidly discarded their military garb, gave up their office work in the military establishments, in order to answer the silent call of their comrades, the millions of Russian workers who even in Soviet Russia drudge out their shamefully miserable existence.

Through their class instinct, these comrades standing at the head of the Workers' Opposition became conscious of the fact that there was something wrong: they understood that even though during these three years we have created the Soviet institutions and reaffirmed the principles of the workers' republic, yet the working class, as a class, as a self-contained social unit with identical class aspirations, tasks, interests, and, hence, with a uniform, consistent, clear-cut policy, becomes an ever less important factor in the affairs of the Soviet republic. Ever less does it lend color to the measures promulgated by its own government; ever less does it direct the policy and influence the work and the trend of thought of the central authorities. During the first period of the revolution, who would dare to speak of the "upper" and the "lower" strata? Masses, namely, the laboring masses, and the leading party centers were all in one. All aspirations that were borne of life and struggle at that time found their most exact reflection in the most clearly defined and scientifically grounded formula of the leading party centers. There was no line drawn between the "upper" and the "lower" strata and there could be none. At present, however, this division does exist, and there is no agitation or intimidation strong enough to eradicate the mass conviction that there has grown up a quite new peculiar social layer — that of the Soviet and "upper" party elements.

The members of the trade unions, the existing nucleus of the Workers' Opposition, have understood this fact, or rather, sensed it by their healthy class instinct. First, they found it necessary to come into close contact with the rank and file. To enter into their class organizations, the unions, which, less than any other institution, have come under the destroying influence of cross-current, foreign, non-proletarian elements, viz., the peasant and bourgeois elements, which by adapting themselves to the Soviet regime deform our Soviet institutions and divert our policy from clearly defined class channels into the morass of "adaptation."

Thus, the Workers' Opposition consists of proletarians closely connected with machine or mine, who are a part and parcel of the working class.

The Workers' Opposition, moreover, is wonderful in that it has no prominent leaders. It originated as any healthy, inevitable, class-founded movement would originate — from the depths of the laboring masses. It sprouted from deep roots simultaneously in all corners of Soviet Russia, when the appearance of the Workers' Opposition in the large centers was not even heard of.

"We had no idea whatever of the fact that in Moscow controversies are taking place," said one delegate from Siberia to one of the Miners' congresses, "and yet questions similar to yours have been agitating our minds also." Behind the Workers' Opposition there stand the proletarian masses, or, to be more exact, the Workers' Opposition is the class-uniform, class-conscious and class-consistent part of our industrial proletariat — that part of it which considers it impossible to substitute the great creative power of the proletariat in the process of building communist economy by the formal label of "the dictatorship of the working class".

The higher we go up the ladder of the Soviet and party hierarchy, the fewer adherents of the Opposition we find. The deeper we penetrate into the masses the more response do we find to the program of the Workers' Opposition. This is very significant, and very important. This must be taken into consideration by the directing centers of our party. If the masses go away from the "upper" elements; if there appears a break, a crack, between the directing centers and the "lower" elements, that means that there is something wrong with the "upper" elements, particularly when the masses are not silent, but think, act, move, and defend themselves and their own slogans.

The "upper" elements may divert the masses from the straight road of history which leads toward communism only when the masses are mute, obedient, and when they passively and credulously follow their leaders. So it was in 1914, at the beginning of the World War, when the workers believed their leaders and decided: "The instinctive feeling of protest against the war deceives us; it is necessary to be silent, to stifle that feeling and obey the superiors." But when the masses are in turmoil, criticize their leaders, and use their own brains; when they stubbornly vote against their beloved leaders, quite often suppressing the feeling of personal sympathy towards them; then the matter assumes a serious turn, and it is the task of the party not to conceal the controversy, not to nick-name the Opposition with unfounded and meaningless epithets, but to ponder seriously over the whole matter and find out where the root of the evil is, where the root of the controversy is, what it is that the working class, the bearer of communism and its only creator, wants. And thus the Workers' Opposition is the advanced part of the proletariat which has not severed the ties with the laboring masses organized into unions, and which has not scattered itself in the Soviet institutions.

The Root Of The Controversy

Before making clear what the cause is of the ever widening break between the "Workers' Opposition" and the official point of view held by our directing centers, it is necessary to call attention to two facts:

(1) The Workers' Opposition sprang from the depths of the industrial proletariat of Soviet Russia, and it is an outgrowth not only of the unbearable conditions of life and labor in which seven millions of the industrial workers find themselves, but is also a product of vacillation, inconsistencies, and outright deviations in our Soviet policy from the clearly expressed class-consistent principles of the communist program.

(2) The Opposition did not originate in some particular center, was not a fruit of personal strife and controversy, but, on the contrary, covers the whole extent of Soviet Russia and meets with a resonant response.

At present there prevails an opinion that the whole root of the controversy arising between the Workers' Opposition and the numerous currents noticeable among the leaders consists exclusively in the difference of opinions regarding the problems that confront the trade unions. This, however, is not true. The break goes deeper. Representatives of the Opposition are not always able to clearly express and define it, but as soon as some vital question of the reconstruction of our republic is touched upon, controversies arise concerning a whole series of cardinal economic and political questions.

For the first time the two different points of view, as they are expressed by the leaders of our party and the representatives of our class-organized workers, found their reflection at the Ninth Congress of our party, when that body was discussing the question: "Collective versus personal management in the industry." At that time there was no opposition from a well-formed group, but it is very significant that collective management was favored by all the representatives of the trade unions, while opposed to it were all the leaders of our party, who are accustomed to appraise all events from the institutional angle. They require a great deal of shrewdness and skill to placate the socially heterogeneous and the sometimes politically hostile aspirations of the different social groups of the population as expressed by proletarians, petty owners, peasantry, and bourgeoisie in the person of specialists, and pseudo-specialists of all kinds and degrees.

Why was it that none but the unions stubbornly defended the principle of collective management, even without being able to adduce scientific arguments in favor of it; and why was it that the specialists' supporters at the same time defended the "one man management"? The reason is that in this controversy, though both sides emphatically denied that there was a question of principle involved, two historically irreconcilable points of view had clashed. The "one man management" is a product of the individualist conception of the bourgeois class. The "one man management" is in principle an unrestricted, isolated, free will of one man, disconnected from the collective.

This idea finds its reflection in all spheres of human endeavor — beginning with the appointment of a sovereign for the state and ending with a sovereign director of the factory. This is the supreme wisdom of bourgeois thought. The bourgeoisie do not believe in the power of a collective body. They like only to whip the masses into an obedient flock, and drive them wherever their unrestricted will desires.

The working class and its spokesmen, on the contrary, realize that the new communist aspirations can be attained only through the collective creative efforts of the workers themselves. The more the masses are developed in the expression of their collective will and common thought, the quicker and more complete will be the realization of working class aspirations, for it will create a new, homogeneous, unified, perfectly arranged communist industry. Only those who are directly bound to industry can introduce into it animating innovations.

Rejection of a principle—the principle of collective management in the control of industry—was a tactical compromise on behalf of our party, an act of adaptation; it was, moreover, an act of deviation from that class policy which we so zealously cultivated and defended during the first phase of the revolution.

Why did this happen? How did it happen that our party, matured and tempered in the struggle of the revolution, was permitted to be carried away from the direct road in order to journey along the round-about path of adaptation, formerly condemned severely and branded as "opportunism."

The answer to this question we shall give later. Meanwhile we shall turn to the question: how did the Workers' Opposition form and develop?

The Ninth Congress (Russian Communist Party) was held in the spring. During the summer the Opposition did not assert itself. Nothing was heard about it during the stormy debates that took place at the Second Congress of the Communist International, but deep at the bottom there was taking place an accumulation of experience, of critical thought. The first expression of this process, incomplete at the time, was at the party conference in September, 1920. For a time the thought preoccupied itself largely with rejections and criticism. The Opposition had no well-formulated proposals of its own. But it was obvious that the party was entering into a new phase of its life. Within its ranks a ferment was at work; signifying that the "lower" elements demand freedom of criticism, loudly proclaiming that bureaucracy strangles them, leaves no freedom for activity, or for manifestation of initiative.

The leaders of the party understood this undercurrent and through comrade Zinoviev made many verbal promises as to freedom of criticism, widening of the scope of self-activity for the masses, persecution of leaders deviating from the principles of democracy, etc. A great deal was said, and said well; but from words to deeds there is a considerable distance. The September conference, together with Zinoviev's much promising speech, has changed nothing either in the party itself or in the life of the masses. The root from which the Opposition sprouts, was not destroyed. Down at the bottom a growth of inarticulate dissatisfaction, criticism, and independence was taking place.

This inarticulate ferment was noted even by the party leaders, where it quite unexpectedly generated sharp controversies. It is significant that in the central party bodies sharp controversies arose concerning the part that must be played by the trade unions. This, however, is only natural.

At present this subject of controversy between the Opposition and the party leaders, while not being the only one, is still the cardinal point of our whole domestic policy.

Long before the Workers' Opposition had appeared with its theses, and formed that basis on which, in its opinion, the dictatorship of the proletariat must rest in the sphere of industrial reconstruction, the leaders in the party had sharply disagreed in their appraisal of the part that is to be played by the working class organizations regarding the latter's participation in the reconstruction of industries on a communist basis. The Central Committee of the party split into groups. Comrade Lenin stood in opposition to Trotsky, while Bukharin took the middle ground.

Only at the Eighth Soviet Congress and immediately after, it became obvious that within the party itself there was a united group kept together primarily by the theses of principles concerning the trade unions. This group, the Opposition, having no great theoreticians, and in spite of a most resolute resistance from the most popular leaders of the party, was growing strong and spreading all over laboring Russia. Was it so only in Petrograd and Moscow? Not at all! Even from the Donetz basin, the Ural Mountains, Siberia, and a number of other industrial centers came reports to the Central Committee that there also the Workers' Opposition was forming and acting. It is true that not everywhere does the Opposition find itself in complete accord on all points with the workers of Moscow. At times there is much indefiniteness, pettiness, and absurdity in the expressions, demands and motives of the Opposition, while even the cardinal points may differ; yet there is everywhere one unalterable point—and this is the question: Who shall develop the creative powers in the sphere of economic reconstruction? Whether purely class organs directly connected by vital ties with the industries—that is, whether industrial unions shall do the work of reconstruction—or shall it be left to the Soviet machine which is separated from direct vital industrial activity and is mixed in its composition? This is the root of the break. The Workers' Opposition defends the first principle, while the leaders of the party, whatever might be their own differences on various secondary matters, are in complete accord on the cardinal point and defend the second principle.

What does this mean?

This means that our party lives through its first serious crisis of the revolutionary period, and that the Opposition is not to be driven away by such a cheap name as "syndicalism," but that all comrades must consider this in all seriousness. Who is right—the leaders, or the working masses endowed with the healthy class instinct?

Crisis In The Party

Before considering the basic points of the controversy between the leaders of our party and the Workers' Opposition, it is necessary to find an answer to the question: How could it happen that our party — formerly strong, mighty, and invincible because of its clear-cut and firm class policy — began to deviate from its program?

The dearer the Communist Party is to us just because it has made such a resolute step forward on the road to the liberation of workers from the yoke of capital, the less right we have to close our eyes to the mistakes of leading centers.

The power of the party must lie in the ability of our leading centers to detect the problems and tasks that confronted the workers, and to pick up the tendencies which they have been able to direct so that the masses might conquer one more of the historical positions. So it was in the past, but it is no longer so at present. Our party not only reduces its speed but ever oftener "wisely" looks back and asks: "Have we not gone too far? Is this not the time to call a halt? Is it not wiser to be more cautious, and to avoid the daring experiments unseen in the whole of the history?"

What was it that produced this "wise caution" (particularly expressed in the distrust of the leading party centers toward the economic industrial abilities of the labor unions), caution that has lately overwhelmed all our centers? Where is the cause?

If we begin diligently to search for the cause of the arising controversy in our party, it becomes clear that the party is passing through a crisis which was brought about by three fundamental causes.

The first main basic cause is the distressful environment in which our party must work and act. The Russian Communist Party must build communism and carry into life its program: (1) In the environment of complete destruction and breakdown of the economic structure. (2) In the face of the never-diminishing ruthless pressure of the imperialist states and white guards. (3) To the working class of Russia has fallen the lot to realize communism, create new communist forms of economy in an economically backward country with a preponderant peasant population, where the necessary economic prerequisites for socialization of production and distribution are lacking, and where capitalism has not been able as yet to complete the full cycle of its development (from the unlimited struggle of competition of the first stages of capitalism to its highest form — to the regulation of production by capitalist unions — the trusts).

It is quite natural that all these factors hinder the practical realization of our program (particularly in its essential part — in the reconstruction of industries on the new basis) and inject into our Soviet economic policy diverse influences and a lack of uniformity.

Out of this basic cause follow the two others. First of all, the economic backwardness of Russia and the domination of the peasantry within its boundaries create that diversity, and inevitably detract the practical policy of our party from the clear-cut class direction, consistent in principle and theory.

Any party standing at the head of a heterogeneous Soviet state is compelled to consider the aspirations of peasants with their petty-bourgeois inclinations and resentments towards communism, as well as lend ear to the numerous petty-bourgeois elements, remnants of the former capitalists in Russia, to all kinds of traders, middlemen, petty officials, etc., who have very rapidly adapted themselves to the Soviet institutions and occupy responsible positions in the centers, appear in the capacity of agents of different commissariats, etc. No wonder that Zurupa, the People's Commissar of Supplies, at the Eighth Congress quoted figures which showed that in the service of the Commissariat of Supplies there were engaged 17 percent of workers, 13 percent of peasants, less than 20 percent of specialists, and that of the remaining, more than 50 percent were "tradesmen, salesmen, and similar people, in the majority even illiterate." (Zurupa's own words.) In Zurupa's opinion this is a proof of their democratic composition, even though they have nothing in common with the class proletarians, with the producers of all wealth, with the workers in factories and mills.

These are the elements—the elements of petty-bourgeois widely scattered through the Soviet institutions, the elements of the middle class with their hostility toward communism, and with their predilections toward the immutable customs of the past, with resentments and fears toward revolutionary acts—these are the elements that bring decay into our Soviet institutions, breeding there an atmosphere altogether repugnant to the working class. They are two different worlds and hostile at that. And yet we in Soviet Russia are compelled to persuade both ourselves and the working class that the petty-bourgeoisie and middle classes (not speaking of well-to-do peasants) can quite comfortably exist under the common motto "All power to the Soviets," forgetful of the fact that in practical everyday life the interests of the workers and those of the middle classes and peasantry imbued with petty-bourgeois psychology must inevitably clash, rending the Soviet policy asunder, and deforming its clear-cut class statutes.

Beside peasant-owners in the villages and burgher elements in the cities, our party in its Soviet state policy is forced to reckon with the influence exerted by the representatives of wealthy bourgeoisie now appearing in the form of specialists, technicians, engineers, and former managers of financial and industrial affairs, who by all their past experience are bound to the capitalist system of production. They cannot even imagine of any other mode of production but only that one which lies within the traditional bounds of capitalist economics.

The more Soviet Russia finds itself in need of specialists in the sphere of technique and management of production, the stronger becomes the influence of these elements, foreign to the working class elements, on the development of our economy. Having been thrown aside during the first period of the revolution, and being compelled to take up an attitude of watchful waiting or sometimes even open hostility toward the Soviet authorities, particularly during the most trying months (the historical sabotage by the intellectuals), this social group of brains in capitalist production, of servile, hired, well-paid servants of capital, acquire more and more influence and importance in politics with every day that passes.

Do we need names? Every fellow worker carefully watching our foreign and domestic policy recalls more than one of such names.

As long as the center of our life remained at the military fronts, the influence of these gentlemen directing our Soviet policy, particularly in the sphere of industrial reconstruction, was comparatively negligible.

Specialists, the remnants of the past, by all their nature closely, unalterably bound to the bourgeois system that we aim to destroy, gradually began to penetrate into our Red Army, introducing there their atmosphere of the past (blind subordination, servile obedience, distinction, ranks, and the arbitrary will of superiors in place of class discipline, etc.), but to the general political activity of the Soviet republic their influence did not extend.

The proletariat did not question their superior skill to direct military affairs, fully realizing through their healthy class instinct that in military matters the working class as a class cannot express a new word, is powerless to introduce substantial changes into the military system—to reconstruct its foundation on a new class basis. Professional militarism—inheritance of the past ages—militarism, wars, will have no place in the communist society. The struggle will go on along other channels, will take quite different forms inconceivable to our imagination. Militarism lives through its last days, through the transitory epoch of dictatorship, and therefore, it is only natural that the workers, as a class, could not introduce into the forms and systems of militarism anything new, and conducive to the future development of society. Even in the Red Army, however, there were innovating touches of the working class, but the nature of militarism remained the same, and the direction of military affairs by the former officers and generals of the old army did not draw the Soviet policy in military affairs away to the opposite side sufficiently for the workers to feel any harm to themselves or to their class interests.

In the sphere of national economy it is quite different, however. Production, its organization—this is the essence of communism. To debar the workers from the organization of industry, to deprive them, that is, their industrial organizations, of the opportunity to develop their powers in creating new forms of production in industry through their unions, to deny these expressions of the class organization of the proletariat, while placing full reliance on the "skill" of specialists trained and taught to carry on production under a quite different system of production—is to jump off the rails of scientific Marxian thought. This is, however, just the thing that is being done by the leaders of our party at present.

Taking into consideration the utter collapse of our industries while still clinging to the capitalist mode of production (payment for labor in money, graduations in wages received according to the work done), our party leaders, in a fit of distrust in the creative abilities of workers' collectives, are seeking salvation from the industrial chaos—where? In the hands of scions of the bourgeois-capitalist past-businessmen and technicians, whose creative abilities in the sphere of industry are subject to the routine, habits and methods of the capitalist system of production and economy. They are the ones who introduce the ridiculously naive belief that it is possible to bring about communism by bureaucratic means. They "decree" where it is now necessary to create and carry on research.

The more the military front recedes before the economic front, the keener becomes our crying need, the more pronounced the influence of that group which is not only inherently foreign to communism, but absolutely unable to develop the right qualities for introducing new forms of organizing the work, of new motives for increasing production, of new approaches to production and distribution. All these technicians, practical men, men of business experience, who just now appear on the surface of Soviet life, by exerting their influence on the economic policy bring pressure to bear upon the leaders of our party through and within the Soviet institutions.

The party, therefore, finds itself in a difficult and embarrassing situation regarding the control over the Soviet state, and is forced to lend ear and adapt itself to three economically hostile groups of the population, each different in social structure. The workers demand a clear-cut, uncompromising policy, a rapid, forced advance toward communism; while the peasantry with its petty-bourgeois proclivities and sympathies demand different kinds of "freedom," including freedom of trade and non-interference into their affairs. The latter are joined in this demand by the burgher class in the form of "agents" of Soviet officials, commissaries in the army, etc. who have already adapted themselves to the Soviet regime, and sway our policy toward petty-bourgeois lines.

As far as the center is concerned, the influence of these petty-bourgeois elements is negligible, but in the provinces and in local Soviet activity their influence is great and a harmful one. Finally, there is still another group of men, that of the former managers and directors of the capitalist industries. These are not the magnates of capital, like Riabushinsky or Rublikoff, whom the Soviet republic got rid of during the first phase of the revolution, but they are the most talented servants of the capitalist system of production, "the brains and genius" of capitalism, its true creators and sponsors. Heartily approving the centralist tendencies of the Soviet government in the sphere of economics, well realizing all the benefits of trustification and regulation of production (this, by the way, is being carried on by capital in all advanced industrial countries), they are striving for just one thing—they want that this regulation should be carried on not through the labor organizations (the industrial unions) but through themselves, acting now under the guise of Soviet economic institutions (the central industrial committees, industrial centers of the Supreme Council of National Economy), where they are already firmly rooted. The influence of these gentlemen on "the sober" state policy of our leaders is great, considerably greater than is desirable. This influence is reflected in the policy which defends and cultivates bureaucratism (with no attempts to change it entirely, but just to improve it). This policy is particularly obvious in the sphere of our foreign trade with the capitalist states, which is just beginning to spring up: the commercial relations are carried on over the heads of the Russian as well as the foreign organized workers. It finds its expression, also, in a whole series of measures restricting the self-activity of the masses and giving the initiative to the scions of the capitalist world.

Among all these various groups of the population our party, by trying to find a middle ground, is compelled to steer a course which would not jeopardize the unity of the state interests. The clear-cut policy of our party in the process of identifying itself with Soviet state institutions is being gradually transformed into an upper-class policy, which in essence is nothing else but an adaptation of our directing centers to the heterogeneous and irreconcilable interests of the socially different mixed population. This adaptation leads to inevitable vacillation, fluctuations, deviations and mistakes. It is only necessary to recall the zigzag-like road of our policy toward the peasantry, which from "banking on the poor peasant" brought us to placing reliance on "the industrious peasant-owner." Let us admit that this policy is proof of the political soberness and "statecraft wisdom" of our directing centers, but the future historian analyzing without bias the stages of our domination will find and point out that in this is evident "a dangerous digression" from the class line toward "adaptation" and a course full of harmful possibilities or results.

Let us take again the question of foreign trade. There exists in our policy an obvious duplicity. This is attested by the constant, unending friction between the Commissariat of Foreign Trade and the Commissariat of Foreign Affairs. This friction is not of administrative nature alone; its cause lies deeper, and if the secret work of the directing centers were exposed to the view of rank and file elements, who knows what the controversy dividing the Commissariat on Foreign Affairs and the trade representatives abroad might lead to?

The seemingly administrative friction that is essentially a serious, deep, social friction, concealed from the rank and file, and makes it absolutely necessary for Soviet politics to adapt itself to the three heterogeneous social groups of the population (workers, peasants, and representatives of the former bourgeoisie), constitutes another cause bringing crisis into our party. And we cannot but pay attention to this cause. It is too characteristic, too pregnant with possibilities. It is, therefore, the duty of our party in behalf of party unity and future activity to ponder over this cause and derive a necessary lesson from the wide-spread dissatisfaction generated by it in the rank and file.

As long as the working class, during the first period of the revolution, felt itself as being the only bearer of communism there was perfect unanimity in the party. In the days immediately following the October revolution none could even think of "ups" as something different from "downs," for in those days the advanced workers were busily engaged in realizing point after point in our class-communist program.

The peasant who received the land did not at that time assert himself as a part of and a full-fledged citizen of the Soviet republic. Intellectuals, specialists, men of affairs—the entire petty-bourgeoisie class and pseudo-specialists climbing at present up the Soviet ladder rung by rung, under the guise of specialists, in watchful waiting stepped aside, giving freedom for the advanced working masses to develop their creative abilities.

At present, however, it is just the other way. The worker feels, sees and realizes at every step that specialists, and, what is still worse, untrained illiterate pseudo-specialists, and practical men, throw out the worker and fill up all the high administrative posts of industrial and economic institutions. And the Party, instead of putting the brakes on this tendency from the elements which are altogether foreign to the working class and communism, encourages it and seeks salvation from the industrial chaos not in the workers, but in these very elements. Not in the workers, not in their union organizations does the Party repose its trust, but in these elements. The working masses feel it, and instead of unanimity and unity in the party there appears a break.

The masses are not blind. Whatever words the most popular leaders might use in order to conceal the deviation from the clear-cut class policy and the compromises made with the peasants and world capitalism, and the trust that they place in the disciples of the capitalist system of production, the working masses feel where the digression begins.

The workers may cherish an ardent affection and love for such personalities as Lenin; they may be fascinated by the incomparable flowery eloquence of Trotsky and his organizing abilities; they may revere a number of other leaders, as leaders, but when the masses feel that they and their class are not trusted, it is quite natural that they say: "No, halt. We refuse to follow you blindly. Let us examine the situation. Your policy of picking out the middle ground between the three socially opposed groups is a wise one indeed but it smacks of the well-tried and familiar adaptation and opportunism. For the present day we may gain something with the help of your sober policy, but let us beware lest we find ourselves on a wrong road that through zig-zags and turns will lead from the future to the debris of the past." Distrust of the leaders toward the workers is steadily growing, and the more sober these leaders are getting, the more clever statesmen they become with their policy of sliding over the blade of a sharp knife between communism and compromise with bourgeoisie past, the deeper becomes the abyss between the "ups" and the "downs," the less understanding there is and the more painful and inevitable becomes the crisis within the party itself.

The third reason enhancing the crisis in the party is that in fact, during these three years of the revolution the economic situation of the working class, of those who work in factories and mills, has not only not been improved, but become more unbearable. This nobody dares to deny. The suppressed and widely-spread dissatisfaction among workers (workers — mind you) has a real justification.

Only the peasants gained directly by the revolution; as far as the middle classes are concerned they very cleverly adapted themselves to the new conditions, together with the representatives of the rich bourgeoisie who had occupied all the responsible and directing positions in the Soviet institutions (particularly in the sphere of directing state economy), in the industrial organizations and the reestablishment of commercial relations with foreign nations. Only the basic class of the Soviet republic which bore all the burdens of the dictatorship as a mass ekes out a shamefully pitiful existence. The workers' republic controlled by the communists, by the vanguard of the working class which, to quote Lenin's words, "has absorbed all the revolutionary energy of the class," has not had time enough to ponder over and improve the conditions of all the workers (those not in individual establishments which happened to gain the attention of the Council of the People's Commissars in one or another of the so-called "shock industries,") but of all the workers in general and lift their conditions of life to a human standard of existence.

The Commissariat of Labor is the most stagnant institution of all the commissariats. In the whole of the Soviet policy there was never seriously raised on a national scale and discussed, the question: what must and can be done in the face of an utter collapse of industry at home and a most unfavorable external situation, in order to improve the workers' conditions and preserve their health for productive labor in the future, and to better the lot of workers in the shops?

Until recently the Soviet policy was devoid of any worked-out plan for improving the lot of the workers and their conditions of life. All that was done in this field was done rather incidentally, or at random, by local authorities under the pressure of the masses themselves. During these three years of civil war the proletariat heroically brought to the altar of the revolution their innumerable sacrifices. They waited patiently, but at present, at the turn of affairs, when the pulse of life in the republic is again transferred to the economic front, the rank and file worker considers it unnecessary "to suffer and wait." Why? Is he not the creator of life on the communist basis? Let us ourselves take up this reconstruction for we know better than the gentlemen from the centers where it hurts us the most.

The rank and file worker is very observant. He sees that so far the problems of hygiene, sanitation, improving conditions of labor in the shops—in other words, the betterment of the workers' lot—has occupied the last place in our policy. Further than housing of workers' families in the inconvenient bourgeois mansions we did not go in our solution of the housing problem, and, what is still worse, so far we have not even touched the practical problem of housing in regard to workers. To our shame, in the heart of the republic, in Moscow itself, they are still living in filthy, overcrowded and unhygienic working men's quarters, one visit to which makes one think that there was no revolution at all. We all know that the housing problem cannot be solved in a few months, even years, and that due to our poverty its solution is confronted with serious difficulties, but the facts of ever growing inequality between the privileged groups of the population in Soviet Russia and the rank and file workers, the "framework of the dictatorship," breed and nourish the dissatisfaction.

The rank and file worker sees how the Soviet official and the practical man lives and how lives he—he on whom rests the dictatorship of the proletariat? He cannot but see that during the revolution the life and health of the workers in the shops commanded the least attention; that where prior to the revolution there existed more or less bearable conditions, they are still maintained by the shop committees, and where the latter did not exist, where dampness, foul air and gases poisoned and destroyed the workers' health, these conditions remained unchanged. "We could not attend to that; pray, there was the military front." And yet whenever it was necessary to make repairs in any of the houses occupied by the Soviet institutions they were able to find both the materials and the labor power. What would happen if we tried to shelter our specialists or practical men engaged in the sphere of commercial transactions with foreign capitalists in those huts in which the masses of workers still live and labor? They would raise such a howl that it would become necessary to mobilize the entire housing department in order to correct "the chaotic conditions" that interfere with the productivity of our specialists.

The service of the Workers' Opposition consists in that it included the problem of improving the workers' lot together with all the other secondary demands of workers into the general economic policy. The productivity of labor cannot be increased unless the life of workers will have been organized on the new communist basis.

The less that is undertaken and planned out (I do not speak of something that has been carried out) in this sphere, the deeper is the misunderstanding, the estrangement, and still greater is the mutual distrust between the directing centers of the party and the rank and file workers. There is no unity, no sense of their identity of needs, demands and aspirations. "The leaders are one thing, and we are something altogether different. Maybe it is true that the leaders know better how to rule over the country, but they fail to understand our needs, our life in the shops, its requirements, and immediate needs; they do not understand, and do not know." From this reasoning follows the instinctive leaning toward the unions, and consequent dropping out of the party. "It is true that they are a part of us, but as soon as they get into the centers, they leave us altogether; they begin to live differently; if we suffer what do they care; our sorrows are not theirs, any longer."

And the more our industrial establishments and unions are drained of their best elements by the party which sends them either to the front or to the Soviet institutions, the weaker becomes the direct connection between the rank and file workers and the directing party centers. A chasm is growing, and at present, therefore, this division manifests itself even in the ranks of the party itself. The workers through their Workers' Opposition ask: Who are we? Are we really the prop of the class dictatorship, or are we just an obedient flock that serves as a support for those who, having severed all ties with the masses, carry out their own policy and build up industry without any regard to our opinions and creative abilities under the reliable cover of the party label?

Whatever the party leaders might do in order to drive away the Workers' Opposition the latter will always remain that growing healthy class force, which is destined to inject vitalizing energy into the rehabilitation of the economic life as well as into the communist party which begins to fade and bend low to the ground.

Thus, there are three causes that bring about a crisis into our party; there are first of all the supreme objective conditions under which communism in Russia is being carried out and realized (the civil war, economic backwardness of the country, its utter industrial collapse as an aftermath of the long years of war); the second cause is the heterogeneous composition of our population (7 millions of workers, the peasantry, the middle classes, and, finally, the former bourgeoisie, men of affairs of all professions, who influence the policy of Soviet institutions and penetrate into the party); the third cause is the inactivity of the party in the field of immediate improvement of the workers' life coupled with the inability and weakness of the corresponding Soviet institutions to take up and solve these problems.

What then is it that the Workers' Opposition wants? What is its service?

If its service consists in that it put up before the party all the perturbing questions, that it gave form to all that heretofore was causing only a subdued agitation in the masses and led the non-partisan workers ever further from the party; that it clearly and fearlessly shouted to the leaders: "Stop, look and think! Where do you lead us? Do we not go off the right road? It will be very bad for the party to find itself without the foundation of the dictatorship, the party will remain by itself, and the working class by itself. In this lies the greatest danger to the revolution."

The task of the party at its present crisis is to fearlessly face the mistakes and lend its ear to the healthy class call of the wide working masses. Through creative powers of the rising class in the form of industrial unions we shall go toward reconstruction and development of creative forces of the country; toward purification of the party itself from the elements foreign to it; toward correction of the activity of the party by means of going back to democracy, freedom of opinion and criticism inside the party.

The Part To Be Played By The Trade Unions, And Their Problems

In a basic yet brief outline we have already explained what it is that causes the crisis in our party. Now we shall make clear what are the most important points of the controversy between the leaders of our party and the Workers' Opposition. There are two such points: The part to be played, and the problems confronting the trade unions during the reconstruction period of the national economy, coupled with the organization of production on the communist basis, and the question of self-activity of the masses coupled with bureaucracy in the party and Soviets.

Let us answer the first question, as the second is the sequence of the first. The period of "making theses" in our party has already ended. Before us we find six different platforms, six party tendencies. Such a variety and such minute variations of shades in its tendencies our party has never seen before, and the party thought has never been so rich in formula on one and the same question. It is, therefore, obvious that the question is a basic one and very important.

And such it is. The whole controversy simmers down to one basic question: Who shall build the communist economy, and how shall it be built? This is, moreover, the essence of our program; this is its heart. This question is not less, if not more important, than the question of seizure of the political state by the proletariat. Only the Bubnoff group of so-called political centralism may be so nearsighted as to underestimate its importance and to say: "The question concerning trade unions at the present moment has no importance whatsoever, and presents none of the theoretical difficulties."

It is, however, quite natural that the question seriously agitates the party as it is in reality the question: in what direction shall we turn the wheel of history—shall we turn it back or move it forward? It is also natural that there is not a single communist in the party who would remain noncommittal during the discussion of this question. As a result we have six different groups.

If we begin, however, to carefully analyze all the theses of these most minutely divergent groups we find that on the basic question—who shall build the communist economy and organize the production on the new basis—there are only two points of view. One is that which is expressed and formulated in the statement of principles of the Workers' Opposition, and the other is one that unites all the rest of the groups, differing only in shades, but identical in substance.

What does the statement of the Workers' Opposition stand for, and how does the latter understand the part that is to be played by the trade unions, or, to be more exact, by the industrial unions at the present moment? "We believe that the question of reconstruction and development of the productive forces of our country may be solved only if the entire system of control over the people's economy is changed." (From Shlyapnikov's report, Dec. 30th). Take notice, comrades, "only if the entire system of control is changed." What does it mean? "The basis of the controversy,"—goes on the report—"revolves around the question: by what means during this period of transformation can our Communist Party carry out its economic policy; whether by means of workers organized into their class unions, or over their heads by bureaucratic means, through canonized functionaries of the state." The basis of the controversy is namely this: whether we shall realize communism through workers or over their heads, by the hands of Soviet officials. And let us, comrades, ponder whether it is possible to attain and build a communist economy by the hands and creative abilities of the scions from the other class, who are imbued with their routine of the past? If we begin to think as Marxians, as men of science, we shall answer categorically and explicitly — no.

The root of the controversy and the cause of the crisis lies in the supposition that "practical men," technicians, specialists and managers of capitalist production can suddenly release themselves from the bonds of their traditional conceptions of ways and means of handling labor, which had been deeply ingrained into their very flesh through the years of their service to capital, and acquire the ability to create new forms of production, of labor organization and of incentives to work.

To suppose that, is to forget the incontestable truth that a system of production cannot be changed by a few individual geniuses, but by the requirements of a class.

Just imagine for a moment that during the transitory period from the feudal system founded on slave labor to the system of capitalist production, with its alleged free hired labor in the industries, (the bourgeois class lacking at that time the necessary experience in the organization of capitalist production), were to invite all the clever, shrewd, experienced managers of the feudal estates who had been accustomed to deal with servile chattel slaves, and entrust to them the task of organizing production on a new capitalist basis. What would happen? Would these specialists in their own sphere, depending on the whip to increase productivity of labor, succeed in handling a "free," though hungry, proletarian, who had released himself from the curse of involuntary labor and had become a soldier or a day laborer? Would not these experts wholly destroy the newly born and developing capitalist production? Individual overseers of the chattel slaves, individual former landlords, and their managers were able to adapt themselves to the new forms of production, but it was not from their ranks that the real creators and builders of the bourgeois capitalist economy were recruited.

The class instinct whispered to the first owners of the capitalist establishments that it is better to go slowly and use common sense in place of experience in search of the new ways and means in establishing relations between capital and labor, than to borrow the antiquated useless methods of exploitation of labor from the old outlawed system. The class instinct quite correctly told the first capitalists during the first period of capitalist development that in place of the whip of the overseer they must apply another incentive: rivalry, personal ambition of workers facing unemployment and misery. And the capitalists, having grasped this new incentive to labor, this new conqueror of labor, were wise enough to use it in order to promote the development of bourgeois capitalist forms of production by increasing the productivity of "free" hired labor to a high degree of intensity.

Five centuries ago the bourgeoisie acted also in a cautious way carefully listening to the dictates of their class instincts. They relied more on their common sense than on the experience of the skillful specialists in the sphere of organizing production on the old feudal estates. The bourgeoisie was perfectly right as history has showed us.

We possess a great weapon that can help us to find the shortest road to the victory of the working class, diminish suffering along the way, and more quickly bring about the new system of production — communism.

This weapon is the materialistic conception of history. However, instead of using it, widening our experience and correcting our researches in conformity with history we are ready to throw this weapon aside, and follow the encumbered circuitous road of blind experiments.

Whatever our economic distress happens to be, we are not justified in going to such an extreme degree of despair, for despair can overcome only the capitalist governments standing with their backs to the wall; after exhausting all the creative impulses of capitalist production they find no solution to their problems.

As far as toiling Russia is concerned, for whom since the October Revolution has been opened new unprecedented opportunities of economic creation, as well as development of new unheard of forms of production, with an immense increase in productivity of labor, there is no room for despair.

It is only necessary not to borrow from the past, but, on the contrary, give complete freedom to the creative powers of the future. This is what the Workers' Opposition is doing. Who can be the builder and the creator of communist economy? That class—and not individual geniuses of the past—which is organically bound with newly developing, painfully born forms of production of a more productive and perfect system of economy. Which organ—the pure class industrial unions, or the heterogeneous Soviet economic establishments—can formulate and solve the creative problems in the sphere of organizing the new economy and its production? The Workers' Opposition considers that it can be done only by the first, that is, by the workers' collective, and not by the functional bureaucratic socially-heterogeneous collective with a strong admixture of elements of the old capitalist type, whose mind is clogged by the refuse of capitalistic routine.

"The workers' unions from the present position of passive assistance to the economic institutions must be drawn into an active participation in the management of the entire economic structure" (The Theses of the Workers' Opposition). To seek, find, and create new and more perfect forms of economy, to find new incentives to the productivity of labor—all this can be done only by the workers' collectives that are closely bound with the new forms of production; only they from their everyday experience may draw certain, at first glance only practically important, and yet exceedingly valuable theoretical conclusions in handling the new labor power in a new labor state where misery, poverty, unemployment and competition on the labor market ceases to be the incentives to labor.

To find a stimulus, an incentive to work—this is the greatest task of the working class standing on the threshold to communism. None other, however, but the working class itself in the form of its class collective is able to solve this great problem.

The solution of this problem, as it is proposed by the industrial unions, consists in giving complete freedom to the workers as regards experimenting, class training, adjusting and feeling out the new forms of production, as well as expression and development of their creative abilities, that is, to that class which alone can be the creator of communism. This is the way the Workers' Opposition handles the solution of this difficult problem from which follows the most essential point of their theses. "Organization of control over the social economy is a prerogative of the All-Russian Congress of producers, who are united in the trade and industrial unions which elect the central body directing the whole economic life of the republic." (Theses of the Workers' Opposition). This point secures freedom for the manifestation of class creative abilities, not restricted and crippled by the bureaucratic machine which is saturated with the spirit of routine of the bourgeois capitalist system of production and control. The Workers' Opposition relies on the creative powers of its own class—the workers. From this premise is deducted the rest of the program.

But right at this point there begins the deviation of the Workers' Opposition from the line that is followed by the party leaders. Distrust toward the working class (not in the sphere of politics, but in the sphere of economic creative abilities) is the whole essence of the theses signed by our party leaders. They do not believe that by the rough hands of workers, untrained technically, can be created those basic outlines of the economic forms from which in the course of time shall develop a harmonious system of communist production.

To all of them—Lenin, Trotsky, Zinoviev and Bukharin—it seems that production is such a "delicate thing" that it is impossible to get along without the assistance of "directors." First of all we shall "bring up" the workers, "teach them," and only when they grow up shall we remove from them all the teachers of the Supreme Council of Natural Economy and let the industrial unions take control over the production. It is, after all, significant that all the theses written by the party leaders coincide in one essential feature: for the present we shall not give control over the production to the trade unions; for the present we "shall wait." It is also true that Trotsky, Lenin, Zinoviev and Bukharin's points of view differ in stating the reason why the workers should not be entrusted with running the industries just at present, but they all unanimously agree that just at the present time the management over the production must be carried on over the workers' heads by means of a bureaucratic system inherited from the past.

On this point all the leaders of our party are in complete accord. "The center of gravitation in the work of the trade unions at the present moment"—assert the "Ten" in their theses—"must be shifted into the economic industrial sphere. The trade unions as class organizations of workers built up in conformity with their industrial functions must take on themselves the major work in organization of production". "Major work" is a too indefinite term which permits of various interpretations, and yet, it would seem, the platform of the "Ten" gives more leeway for the trade unions in running the industries than Trotsky centralism. Is this the case, however? Further, the theses of the Ten go on to explain what they mean by "major work" of the unions. "The most energetic participation in the centers which regulate production and control, register and distribute labor power, organize exchange between cities and villages, fight against sabotage and carry out decrees on different compulsory labor obligations, etc." This is all. Nothing new and nothing more than what the trade unions have already been doing, and which cannot save our production nor help in the solution of the basic question — raising and developing the productive forces of our country.

In order to make clear the fact that the program of the "Ten" does not give to the trade unions any of the directing functions, but assigns to them only an auxiliary role in the management of production, the authors of it say: "In a developed stage (not at present, but in a developed stage) the trade unions in their process of social revolution must become organs of the social authority, working as such, in subordination to other organizations, toward carrying out the new principles of organization of the economic life." By this they meant to say that the trade unions must work in subordination to the Supreme Council of National Economy and its branches. What is the difference then with that and "joining by growth" which was proposed by Trotsky? The difference is only in methods. The theses of the "Ten" strongly emphasize the educational nature of the trade unions. In their formulation of problems for the trade unions, mainly in the sphere of organization, industry and education, our party leaders as clever politicians suddenly convert themselves into "teachers."

This peculiar controversy is revolving not around the system of management in industry, but mainly around the system of bringing up the masses. In fact when one begins to turn over the pages of the stenographic minutes and speeches made by our prominent leaders, one is astonished by the unexpected manifestation of their pedagogic proclivities. Every author of the theses proposes the most perfect system of bringing up the masses, but all these systems of "education" lack provisions for freedom of experiment, for training and expressing creative abilities by those who are to be taught; in this respect all our pedagogues are also behind the times.

The trouble is that Lenin, Trotsky, Bukharin and others limit the functions of the trade unions not to the control over production or taking over the industries, but to a mere school of bringing up the masses. During the discussion to some of our comrades it seemed that Trotsky stands for a gradual "absorption of the unions by the state" — not all of a sudden, but gradual, and wants to reserve for them the right of ultimate control over production, as it is expressed in our program. This point, it seemed at first, put Trotsky on a common ground with the Opposition at a time when the group represented by Lenin and Zinoviev, being opposed to "the absorbtion by the state," sees the object of the union activity and their problem in "training for communism." "Trade unions" — thunder Trotsky and Zinoviev — "are necessary for the rough work" (page 22 of the Report, Dec. 30th). Trotsky himself, it would seem, understands the task somewhat differently; in his opinion the most important work of the unions consists in organizing production. In this he is perfectly right; he is also right when he says: "Inasmuch as unions are schools of communism they are such schools not in carrying on general propaganda (for in such a case they would play the part of clubs), not in mobilizing their members for military work or collecting the produce tax, but for the purpose of all-round education of their members on the basis of their participation in production." (Trotsky's report, December 30th). All this is true, but there is one grave omission; the unions are not only schools for communism, but they are its creators as well.

Creativeness of the class is being lost sight of. Trotsky substitutes it by initiative of "the real organizers of production," by communists inside the unions (from Trotsky's report, Dec. 30th). What communists? According to Trotsky, those communists who are appointed by the party to responsible administrative positions into the unions for reasons that quite often have nothing in common with considerations of industrial and economic problems of the unions. Trotsky is frank. He does not believe in workers' preparedness to create communism, and through pain and suffering to seek, to blunder, and still create new forms of production. He has expressed this frankly and openly. He has already carried out his system of "club education" of the masses, and of their training for the role of "master" in the Central Administrative body of Railways by adopting all those methods of educating the masses which were practiced by our traditional journeymen upon their apprentices. It is true that a beating on the head by a boot stretcher does not make an apprentice a successful shop-keeper after he becomes a journeyman, and yet as long as the boss-teacher's stick hangs over his head he works and produces.

This, in Trotsky's opinion, is the whole essence of shifting the central point "from politics to industrial problems." To raise even temporarily productivity by every and all means is the whole crux of the task. Toward this end must be, in Trotsky's opinion, also directed the whole course of training in the trade unions.

Comrades Lenin and Zinoviev, however, disagree with him. They are "educators" of "a modern trend of thought." It has been stated many a time that the trade unions are schools for communism. What does that mean — "schools for communism"? If we take this definition seriously, it will mean that in school for communism it is necessary first of all to teach and bring up, but not to command (this allusion to Trotsky's views meets with applauses). Further on Zinoviev adds: the trade unions are performing a great task both for the proletarian and communist cause. This is the basic part to be played by the trade unions. At present, however, we forget this, and think that we may handle the problem of trade unions too recklessly, too roughly, too severely.

It is necessary to remember that these organizations have their own particular tasks — not of commanding, supervising or dictating, but tasks in which all may be reduced to one — drawing of the working masses into the channel of the organized proletarian movement. Thus, teacher Trotsky went too far in his system of bringing up the masses, but what does comrade Zinoviev himself propose? To give within the unions the first lessons in communism, "to teach them (the masses) the elementals of the proletarian movement." How? "Through practical experience, through practical creation of the new forms of production" (just what the opposition wants)? Not at all. Zinoviev-Lenin's group favors a system of bringing up through reading, giving moral precepts and good, well-chosen examples. We have 500,000 communists (among whom, we regret to say, there are many "strangers"—stragglers from the other world) to 7,000,000 workers.

According to comrade Lenin the party has drawn into itself "the proletarian vanguard," and the best communists, in co-operation with specialists from the Soviet economic institutions, are searching hard in their laboratories for the new forms of communist production. These communists working at present under the care of "good teachers" in the Supreme Council of National Economy or other centers, these Peters and Johns are the best pupils, it is true, but the working masses in the trade unions must look to these exemplary Peters and Johns and learn something from them without touching with their own hands the rudder of control, for it is too early as yet, as they have not learned enough.

In Lenin's opinion, the trade unions, that is, the working class organizations, are not the creators of the communist forms of people's economy, for they serve only as a connecting link of the vanguard with the masses—"the trade unions in their everyday work persuade masses, masses of that class . . ." etc.

This is not Trotsky's "club system," not a medieval system of education. This is the Froebel-Pestalozzi's German system founded on studying examples. Trade unions must do nothing vital in the industries, but to persuade masses, and keep the masses in touch with the vanguard, with the party, which (remember this!) does not organize production as a collective, but only creates the Soviet economic institutions of a heterogeneous composition, and whereto it appoints communists.

Which system is better?—this is the question. Trotsky's system, whatever it may be in other respects, is clearer, and, therefore, more real. On reading books and studying examples taken from good-hearted Peters and Johns one cannot advance education too far. This must be remembered, and remembered well.

Bukharin's group occupied the middle ground or, rather, attempts to coordinate both systems of bringing up; we must notice, however, that this also does not recognize the principle of independent creativeness of the unions in industry. In the opinion of Bukharin's group the trade unions play a double role (so it is proclaimed in its theses); on one hand it (obviously "the role") takes on itself the functions of a "school for communism," and, on the other hand, the functions of an intermediary between the party and the masses (this is from Lenin's group); it takes, in other words, the role of a machine injecting the wide proletarian masses into the active life (notice, comrades — "into the active life", but not into the creation of the new form of economy, and search for new forms of production). Besides that, they (obviously the unions) in ever increasing degree must become the component part both of the economic machine and the state authority. This is from Trotsky's "joining together."

The controversy again revolves not around the trade union problems, but around the methods of educating the masses by means of unions. Trotsky stands, or rather, stood for, a system which, with the help of that introduced among the railway workers, might hammer into the organized workers' heads the wisdom of communist reconstruction, and by means of "appointees," "shake-ups," and all kinds of miraculous measures promulgated in conformity with "the shock system", could remake the unions so that they might join the Soviet economic institutions by growth and become obedient tools in realizing economic plans worked out by the Supreme Council of National Economy.

Zinoviev and Lenin are not in a hurry to join the trade unions to the Soviet economic machine. The unions, they say, shall remain unions. As regards production it will be run and managed by men whom we choose. When the trade unions have brought up obedient and industrious Peters and Johns we will "inject" them into the Soviet economic institutions and thus the unions will gradually disappear, dissolve.

The creation of new forms of national economy we entrust to the Soviet bureaucratic institutions; as to the unions we leave to them the role of "schools." Education, education, and more education. Such is the Lenin-Zinoviev slogan. Bukharin, however, wanted "to bank" on radicalism in the system of union education, and, of course, fully merited the rebuke from Lenin together with the nickname of "Simidicomist." Bukharin and his group, while emphasizing the educational part to be played by the unions in the present political situation, stand for the most complete workers' democracy inside the unions, for wide elective powers to the unions — not only for the elective principle generally applied, but for non-conditional election of delegates nominated by the unions. Pray, what a democracy! This smacked of the very Opposition itself, if it were not for one difference. The Workers' Opposition sees in the unions the managers and creators of the communist economy whereas Bukharin together with Lenin and Trotsky leave to them only the role of "schools for communism," and no more. Why should he not play with the elective principle when everybody knows that it will do no good or bad for the system of running the industry? For, as a matter of fact, the control over the industry will still remain outside the unions, beyond their reach, in the hands of the Soviet institutions. Bukharin reminds us of those teachers who carry on education in conformity with the old system by means of "books." — "You must learn that far, and no further", while encouraging "self-activity" of the pupils in organizing dances, entertainments, etc.

In this way the two systems quite comfortably live together, and square one with another. But what the outcome of all this will be, and what duties will the pupils of these teachers of eclectics be able to perform — this is a different question. If comrade Lunacharsky were to disapprove at all the educational meetings "eclectic heresy" like this the position of the People's Commissariat on Education would be precarious, indeed.

However, there is no need to underestimate the educational methods of our leading comrades in regard to the trade unions. They all, Trotsky included, realize that in the matter of education "self-activity" of the masses is not the least factor. Therefore, they are in search of such a plan where the trade unions without any harm to the prevailing bureaucratic system of running the industry, may develop their initiative and their economic creative powers. The least harmful sphere where the masses could manifest their self-activity as well as their "participation in active life" (according to Bukharin) is the sphere of betterment of the workers' lot. The Workers' Opposition pays a great deal of attention to this question, and yet it knows that the basic sphere of class creation is the creation of new industrial economic forms, of which the betterment of the workers' lot is only a part.

In Trotsky and Zinoviev's opinion the production must be created and adjusted by the Soviet institutions while the trade unions are advised to perform a rather restricted, though useful, work of improving the lot of the workers. Comrade Zinoviev, for instance, sees in distribution of clothing the "economic role" of the unions and explains: "there is no other more important problem than that of economy; to repair one bath house in Petrograd at present is ten times more important than delivering five good lectures."

What is this? A naive mistaken view, or a conscious substitution of organizing creative tasks in the sphere of production, and development of creative abilities by restricted tasks of home economics, house-hold duties, etc? In somewhat different language the same thought is expressed by Trotsky. He very generously proposes to the trade unions to develop the greatest initiative possible in the economic field.

But where shall this initiative express itself? In "putting glasses" in the shop window or filling up a pool in front of the factory (from Trotsky's speech at the Miner's Congress). Comrade Trotsky, take pity on us! For this is merely the sphere of "house-running," and if you intend to reduce the creativeness of the unions to such a scope then the unions will become not schools for communism, but places where they train people for janitors. It is true that comrade Trotsky attempts to widen the scope of the "self-activity of the masses" by letting them participate not in an independent improvement of the workers' lot on the job (that far goes only the "insane" Workers' Opposition), but by taking lessons from the Supreme Council of National Economy on this subject.

Whenever a question concerning workers is to be decided, as, for instance, about distribution of food or labor power, it is necessary that the trade unions must know exactly (not participate themselves in the matter, but only know), not in general outline, as mere citizens, but know thoroughly the whole current work that is being done by the Supreme Council of National Economy (speech of Dec. 30th). The teachers from the Supreme Council of National Economy not only force the trade unions "to carry out" their plans, but they also "explain to their pupils their decrees." This is already a step forward in comparison with the system that functions at present on the railways.

To every thinking worker it is clear, however, that putting in glasses, being as useful as it may, has nothing in common with running the industry. Productive forces and their development do not find expression in this work. The really important question still is: how to develop them, how to build such a state of economy by squaring the new life with production, in order to eliminate the unproductive labor as much as possible. A party may bring up a red soldier, a political worker, or executive worker to carry out the projects already laid out, but it cannot develop a creator of communist economy, for only a union offers an opportunity for developing the creative abilities along new lines.

Moreover, this is not the task of the party. The party task is to create conditions, that is, give freedom to the working masses united by common economic industrial aims, so that they could bring up a worker-creator, find new impulses for work, could work out a new system to utilize labor power, and might know how to distribute workers in order to reconstruct society, and thus to create a new economic order of things founded on the communist basis. Only workers can generate in their mind new methods of organizing labor as well as running industry.

This is a simple Marxian truth, and yet at present the leaders of our party do not share it with us. Why? Just because they place more reliance on the bureaucratic technicians, descendants of the past, than in the healthy elemental class creativeness of the working masses. In every other sphere we may hesitate as to who is to be in the control—whether the workers' collective or the bureaucratic specialists, be that in the matter of education, developing of science, organization of the army, care of public health, but there is one place, that of the economy, where the question as to who shall have the control is very simple and clear for everyone who has not forgotten history.

It is well known to every Marxian that reconstruction of industry and development of creative forces of a country depend on two factors: on the development of technique, and the efficient organization of labor by means of increasing productivity and finding new incentives to work. This has been true during every period of transformation from a lower stage of economic development to one higher throughout all the history of human existence.

In a labor republic, the development of productive forces by means of technique plays a secondary role in comparison with the second factor, that of the efficient organization of labor, and creation of a new system of economy. Even if Soviet Russia succeeds in carrying out completely its project of general electrification without introducing any essential change in the system of control and organization of the people's economy and production, it would only catch up with the advanced capitalist countries in the matter of development.

Yet, in the efficient utilization of labor power and building up a new system of production Russian labor finds itself in exceptionally favorable circumstances, which give her the opportunity to leave far behind all the bourgeois capitalist countries in the matter of developing the productive forces. Unemployment as an incentive to labor in Soviet Russia has been done away with. Therefore, there are open new possibilities for the working class that had been freed from the yoke of capital, to say its own new creative word in finding new incentives to labor and creation of new forms of production which will have had no precedent in all human history.

Who can, however, develop the necessary creativeness and keenness in this sphere? Whether bureaucratic elements, heads of the Soviet institutions or the industrial unions whose members in their experience in regrouping workers in the shop come across creative, useful, practical methods that can be applied in the process of reorganizing the entire system of the people's economy? The Workers' Opposition asserts that administration of the people's economy is the trade unions' job, and, therefore, it is more Marxian in thought than the theoretically trained leaders.

The Workers' Opposition is not so ignorant as to wholly underestimate the great value of the technical progress or the usefulness of technically trained men. It does not, therefore, think that after electing its own body of control over the industry it may safely dismiss the Supreme Council of National Economy, the central industrial committees, economic centers, etc. Not at all. And yet the Workers' Opposition thinks that it must assert its own control over these technically valuable administrative centers, give them theoretical tasks, and use their services as the capitalists did when they hired the technicians in order to carry out their own schemes. Specialists indeed can do valuable work in developing the industries; they can make the workers' manual labor easier; they are necessary, indispensable, as science is indispensable to every rising and developing class, but the bourgeois specialists, even with the "communist" label pasted on, are powerless physically and too weak mentally to develop productive forces in a non-capitalist state; to find new methods of labor organization, and develop new incentives for intensification of labor.

In this, the last word belongs to the working class—to the industrial unions.

When the class of rising bourgeoisie, having reached the threshold leading from medieval to modern times, entered into the economic battle with the decaying class of feudal lords it did not possess any of the technical advantages over the latter. The trader—the first capitalist—was compelled to buy goods from that craftsman or journeyman who by means of hand files, knife and primitive spindles was producing goods both for his "master," the landlord, and for the outside trader, with whom he entered into a "free" trade agreement. Feudal economy having reached a culminating point in its organization, ceased to give any surplus, and there began a decrease in the growth of productive forces; humanity stood face to face with an alternative of either economic decay or of finding new incentives for labor, of creating, consequently, a new economic system which would increase productivity, widen the scope of production, and open new possibilities for the development of productive forces.

Who could have found and evolved the new methods in the sphere of industrial reorganization? None but those class representatives who had not been bound by the routine of the past, who understood that the spindle and cutter in the hands of a chattel slave produce incomparably less than in the hands of supposedly free hired workers behind whose back stands the incentive of economic necessity.

Thus, the rising class having found where the basic incentive to labor lies, has built on it a complex system great in its own way; the system of capitalist production. The technicians have come to the aid of capitalists only much later. The basis was the new system of labor organization, and the new relations that were established between capital and labor.

The same is true at present. No specialist or technician imbued with the routine of the capitalist system of production can ever introduce any new creative motive and vitalizing innovation into the fields of labor organization, in creating and adjusting the communist economy. Here the function belongs to the workers' collective. The great service of the Workers' Opposition is that it has put up this quest1on of supreme importance frankly and openly before the party. Comrade Lenin considers that we can put through the communist plan on the economic field by means of the party. Is it so? First of all let us consider how the party functions. According to comrade Lenin, "it attracts to itself the vanguard of workers"; then it scatters it over various Soviet institutions (only a part of the vanguard gets back into the trade unions, where the communist members, however, are deprived of an opportunity of directing and building up the people's economy). There these well trained, faithful, and, perhaps, very talented communist-economists disintegrate and decay in the general atmosphere of routine which pervades all our Soviet economic institutions. In such an atmosphere the influence of these comrades is weakened, marred or entirely lost.

Quite a different thing with the trade unions. There the class atmosphere is thicker, the composition of forces is more homogeneous, the tasks that the collective is faced with are more closely bound with the immediate life and labor needs of the producers themselves, of the members of factory and shop committees, of the factory management, and the unions' centers. Creativeness, research of new forms for production, for new incentives to labor, in order to increase productivity, may be generated only in the bosom of this natural class collective. Only the vanguard of the class can create revolution, but only the whole class can create through everyday experience and practical work of its basic class collective.

Whoever does not believe in the creative spirit of a class collective—and this collective is most fully represented by the trade union—must put a cross over the communist reconstruction of society. Neither can Krestinsky or Preobrajznsky nor Lenin and Trotsky push to the forefront by the means of their party machine, without a mistake, those workers who are able to find and point out new approaches to the new system of production. Such workers can be advanced only by life-experience itself from the ranks of those who actually produce and organize production at the same time.

Nevertheless, this consideration, very simple and clear to every practical man, is lost sight of by our party leaders. It is impossible to decree communism. It can be created only in the process of practical research, through mistakes, perhaps, but only by the creative powers of the working class itself.

The cardinal point of controversy that is taking place between the party leaders and the Workers' Opposition is this: In whom will our party place the trust of building up the communist economy — in the Supreme Council of National Economy with all its bureaucratic branches, or in the Industrial Unions? Comrade Trotsky wants "to join" the trade unions to the Supreme Council of People's Economy so that with the assistance of the latter it might be possible to swallow the first. Comrades Lenin and Zinoviev, on the other hand, want to "bring up" masses to such a level of communist understanding that they could be painlessly absorbed into the same Soviet institutions. Bukharin and the rest of the factions express essentially the same view, and the variation consists only in the way they put it, the essence is the same. Only the Workers' Opposition expresses something entirely different, defends the class proletarian viewpoint in the very process of creation and realization of its tasks.

The administrative economic body in the labor republic during the present transitory period must be a body directly elected by the producers themselves. All the rest of the administrative economic Soviet institutions shall serve only as executive centers of the economic policy of that all-important economic body of the labor republic. All else is a goose-stepping that manifests distrust toward the creative abilities of workers, distrust which is not compatible with the professed ideals of our party, whose very strength depends on the perennial revolutionary creative spirit of the proletariat.

There will be nothing surprising if at the approaching party congress the sponsors of the different economic reforms, save the single exception of the Workers' Opposition, will come to a common understanding through mutual compromises and concessions since there is no essential controversy among them.

The Workers' Opposition alone will not and must not compromise. This does not, however, mean that it "drives to a split." Not at all. Its task is entirely different. Even in the event of defeat at the congress it must remain in the party, and step by step stubbornly defend its point of view, save the party, and clarify its class lines.

Once more in brief: what is it that the Workers' Opposition wants?

1) To form a body from the workers—producers themselves—for administering the people's economy.

2) For this purpose, viz.: for the transformation of the unions from the role of passive assistance to the economic bodies, to that of an active participation and manifestation of their creative initiative, the Workers' Opposition proposes a series of preliminary measures to an orderly and gradual realization of this aim.

3) Transferring of the administrative functions of industry into the hands of the union does not take place until the All-Russian Central Executive Committee of the trade unions has found said unions as being able and sufficiently prepared for the task.

4) All appointments to the administrative economic positions shall be made with consent of the union. All candidates nominated by the union are non-removable. All responsible officials appointed by the union are responsible to, and may be recalled by, it.

5) In order to carry out all these proposals it is necessary to strengthen the rank and file nucleus in the unions, and to prepare factory and shop committees for running the industries.

6) By means of concentrating in one body the entire administration of the public economy (without the existing dualism of the Supreme Council of National Economy and the All-Russian Executive Committee of the trade unions) there must be created a oneness of will that will make it easy to carry out the plan and put into life the communist system of production. Is this "syndicalism"? Is not this, on the contrary, the same as what is stated in our party program, and are not the statements of principles signed by the rest of the comrades deviating from it?

On Bureaucracy And Self-Activity Of The Masses

Whether it be bureaucracy, or self-activity of the masses? This is the second point of the controversy between the leaders of our party and the Workers' Opposition. The question of bureaucracy was raised and only superficially discussed at the 8th Soviet Congress. Herein, just as in the question on the part to be played by the trade unions and their problems, the discussion was shifted to a wrong channel. The controversy on this question is more fundamental than it might seem. The essence of it is this: what system of administration in a workers' republic during the period of creation of the economic basis for communism secures more freedom for the class creative powers — whether a bureaucratic state system or a system of wide practical self-activity of the working masses? The question relates to the system of administration, and the controversy arises between two diametrically opposed principles — bureaucracy or self-activity. And yet they try to squeeze it into the scope of the problem that concerns itself only with the methods of "animating the Soviet institutions." Here we observe the same substitution of the subjects discussed, as the one that occurred in the debates on the trade unions. It is necessary to state definitely and clearly that half-measures, changes in relations between central bodies, local economic organizations, and other such petty non-essential innovations as replacing responsible officials or injecting party members into the Soviet institutions, where these communists are subjected to all the bad influences of the prevailing bureaucratic system, and disintegrate among the elements of the former bourgeois class, will not bring "democratization" or life into the Soviet institutions.

This is not the thing, however. Every child in Soviet Russia knows that the vital problem is to draw the wide toiling masses of workers, peasants, and others into the reconstruction of economy in the proletarian state, and change the conditions of life accordingly, in other words the task is clear: to wake up initiative and self-activity in the masses. But what is being done in order to encourage and develop that initiative? Nothing at all. Quite the contrary. It is true that at every meeting we call upon the working men and women "to create a new life, build up, and assist the Soviet authorities," but no sooner do the masses or individual groups of workers take our admonition seriously and attempt to carry it out into life than some of the bureaucratic institutions, feeling that they are being ignored, are in haste to cut short the efforts of too zealous initiators.

Every comrade can easily recall scores of instances when workers themselves attempted to organize dining rooms, day nurseries for children, transportation of wood, etc., and when each time a lively immediate interest in the undertaking died from the red tape, interminable negotiations with various institutions that brought no definite results, or refusals, new requests, etc. Wherever there was an opportunity under impetus of the masses themselves, the masses by their own efforts, to equip a dining room, to store a supply of wood or to organize a nursery, refusal always followed; refusal from the central institutions with explanations that there was no equipment for the dining room, lack of horses for transporting the wood, and absence of an adequate building for the nursery. And how much bitterness is generated among working men and women when they see and know that if they had been given the right, and an opportunity to act, they themselves would put the project through. How painful it is to receive a refusal of necessary materials when they had already been found and procured by the workers themselves. Therefore, the initiative is slackening and the desire to act is dying out. If that is the case "let officials themselves take care of us." As a result there is generated a most harmful division: we are the toiling people, and they are the Soviet officials, on whom everything depends. This is the whole trouble.

Meanwhile, what are our party leaders doing? Do they attempt to find the cause of the evil, and to admit openly that the very system itself, which was carried out into the life through the Soviets, paralyzes and deadens the masses, though it was meant to encourage their initiative? No, our party leaders do nothing of the kind. Just the opposite—instead of finding means to encourage the mass initiative which shall perfectly fit into our flexible Soviet institutions under certain conditions, our party leaders all of a sudden appear in the role of defenders and knights of bureaucracy. How many comrades, while following Trotsky's example, repeat that "we suffer not because of adopting the bad sides of bureaucracy but just because we have failed so far to learn the good ones." ("On One Common Plan," by Trotsky.)

Bureaucracy, as it is, is a direct negation of mass self-activity, and, therefore, whoever accepts the principle of attracting the masses to an active participation in directing the affairs as a basis for the new system in the labor republic cannot look for good or bad sides in bureaucracy, but must openly and resolutely reject this useless system. Bureaucracy is not a product of our misery, as comrade Zinoviev tries to convince, neither is it a reflex of "the blind subordination" to superiors generated by militarism, as others assert. This phenomenon has a deeper cause. It is a by-product of the same cause that explains our policy of double-dealing toward the trade unions: the growing influence in the Soviet institutions of those elements which are hostile in spirit not only to communism, but to the elementary aspirations of the working masses as well. Bureaucracy is a scourge that pervades the very marrow of our party as well as of the Soviet institutions, and this fact is emphasized not only by the Workers' Opposition but is also recognized by many thoughtful comrades not belonging to this group.

The restrictions on initiative are put not only in regard to the activity of non-partisan masses (this would be only a logical and reasonable condition in the suppressed atmosphere of the civil war), the initiative of party members themselves is also restricted. Every independent attempt, every new thought that had not passed through the censorship of our center is considered as "heresy," as a violation of the party discipline, as an attempt to infringe on the prerogatives of the center, which must "foresee" everything, and "decree" anything and everything. If anything is not decreed one must wait, for the time will come when the center at its leisure will decree, and then within sharply restricted limits one may express his "initiative." What would happen if some of the members of the Russian Communist Party — those, for instance, who are very fond of birds — decided to form a society for preservation of birds. The idea itself seems very useful, and does not in any way undermine the "state projects," but it only seems this way. All of a sudden there would appear some bureaucratic institution, and claim its right to the management of that particular undertaking; that institution would immediately "incorporate" the society into the Soviet machine, deadening, thereby, the direct initiative; and instead of it there would appear a heap of paper decrees and regulations which would give enough work for other hundreds of officials and more complicate the work of mails and transport.

The harm in bureaucracy lies not only in the red tape, as some comrades would want us to believe when they narrow the whole controversy to the "animation of Soviet institutions," but also in the solution of all problems not by means of an open exchange of opinions or by immediate efforts of all concerned, but by means of formal decisions handed down from the central institutions, and arrived at either by one person or by an extremely restricted collective, wherein the interested people quite often are absent entirely. Some third person decides your fate, this is the whole essence of bureaucracy.

In the face of the growing suffering in the working class brought about by the confusion of the present transitory period, bureaucracy finds itself particularly weak and impotent. The miracle of enthusiasm in stimulating the productive forces and alleviating the labor conditions can be performed only by the animated initiative of the interested workers themselves, not restricted and repressed at every step by a hierarchy of "permissions and decrees."

All Marxians, Bolsheviks in particular, have been strong and powerful in that they never stressed the policy of immediate success of the movement (this line, by the way, has always been followed by the opportunists-compromisers), but always attempted to put the workers in such conditions which would give them the opportunity to temper their revolutionary will, and develop the creative abilities. The workers' initiative is indispensable for us, and yet we do not give it a chance to develop.

Fear of criticism and freedom of thought by combining together with bureaucracy quite often produce ridiculous forms.

There can be no self-activity without freedom of thought and opinion, for self-activity manifests itself not only in initiative, action, and work, but in independent thought as well. We are afraid of mass-activity. We are afraid to give freedom to the class activity, we are afraid of criticism, we have ceased to rely on the masses, hence, we have bureaucracy with us. That is why the Workers' Opposition considers that bureaucracy is our enemy, our scourge, and the greatest danger for the future existence of the Communist Party itself.

In order to do away with the bureaucracy that is finding its shelter in the Soviet institutions, we must first of all get rid of all bureaucracy in the party itself. That is where we face the immediate struggle against this system. As soon as the party — not in theory but in practice — recognizes self-activity of the masses as the basis of our state, the Soviet institutions will again automatically become those living institutions which are destined to carry out the communist project, and will cease to be the institutions of red tape, laboratories for dead-born decrees, into which they had very rapidly degenerated.

What shall we do, then, in order to destroy bureaucracy in the party and introduce in it the workers' democracy? First of all it is necessary to understand that our leaders are wrong when they say: "Just now we agree to let the reins loose somewhat," for there is no immediate danger on the military front, but as soon as we shall feel again the danger, we will go back to "the military system" in the party. They are not right because we must remember that heroism saved Petrograd, more than once defended Lugansk, other centers, and whole regions. Was it the Red Army alone that put up the defense? No, there was besides the heroic self-activity and initiative of the masses themselves. Every comrade will recall that during the moments of supreme danger the party always appealed to the self-activity of the masses, for it saw in them the anchor of salvation. It is quite true that at times of threatening danger the party and class discipline must be more strict, there must be more self-sacrifice, exactitude in performing duties, etc., but between these manifestations of the class spirit and "the blind subordination" that is being developed lately by the party there is a great difference.

The Workers' Opposition together with a group of responsible workers in Moscow, in the name of party regeneration and elimination of bureaucracy from the Soviet institutions, demands complete realization of all democratic principles, not only for the present period of respite, but also for times of internal and external tension. This is the first and basic condition of the party regeneration, of its return to the principles of the program from which in practice it is more and more deviating under the pressure of elements that are foreign to it.

The second condition, fulfillment of which with all determination is insisted upon by the Workers' Opposition, is the expulsion from the party of all non-proletarian elements. The stronger becomes the Soviet authority the greater is the number of middle class, and sometimes even openly hostile elements, joining the party. The elimination of these elements must be complete and thorough, and those in charge of it must take into account the fact that all the most revolutionary elements from the non-workers had joined the party during the first period of the October revolution. The party must become a workers' party, for only then will it be able to repeal with force all the influences that are being brought to bear upon it by the petty-bourgeois elements, peasants, or by the faithful servants of capital — the specialists.

The Workers' Opposition proposes to register all members who are non-workers and who had joined the party since 1919, and reserve for them the right to appeal within three months from the decisions arrived at, in order that they might join the party again.

At the same time it is necessary to establish "a working status" for all non-working elements which will try to get back into the party, by providing that every applicant to membership in the party must have worked a certain period of time at manual labor under general working conditions before he becomes eligible for enrollment into the party.

The third decisive step toward democratization of the party is the elimination of all non-workers elements from all the administrative positions; in other words, the central, provincial, and county committees of the party must be composed so that workers closely connected with the working masses would have the preponderant majority therein.

In close connection with this point of the Oppositions' demands stands the other of converting all our party centers, beginning from the Central Executive Committee and including the provincial county committees, from institutions taking care of routine, everyday work, into institutions of control over the Soviet policy.

We have already remarked that the crisis in our party is a direct outcome of the three distinct cross-current tendencies that correspond to the three different social groups, viz.: the working class, the peasantry together with the middle class, and the elements of former bourgeoisie, that is, specialists, technicians, and men of affairs.

The problems of state-wide importance compel both the local and central Soviet institutions, including even the Council of People's Commissars and the All-Russian Central Executive Committee, to lend ear to and conform with these three distinct tendencies of the groups that compose the population of Soviet Russia; as a result the class line of the general policy is blurred, and the necessary stability is lost. Considerations of the state interests begin to outweigh the interests of workers.

In order that the Central Committee and party committees may stand firmly on the side of our class policy, and call all our Soviet institutions to order each time that a decision in the Soviet policy becomes obvious (as it happened, for instance, in the question dealing with the trade unions), it is necessary to disassociate the prerogatives of such responsible officials who at one and the same time fill up responsible posts both in the Soviet institutions and in the Communist Party centers. We must remember that Soviet Russia so far has not been a socially homogeneous unit, but, on the contrary, represented a heterogeneous social conglomeration, and, therefore, the state authority is compelled to reconcile all these at times even hostile interests by choosing the middle ground.

In order that the Central Committee of our party could become the supreme directing center of our class policy, the organ of class thought and control over the practical policy of the Soviets, and the spiritual personification of our basic program it is necessary, particularly in the Central Committee, to restrict to a minimum the multiple office holding by those who, while being members of the Central Committee, occupy high posts in the Soviet government. For this purpose the Workers' Opposition proposes formation of party centers, which would really serve as organs of ideal control over the Soviet institutions, and would direct their actions along clear-cut class policies. Moreover, in order to increase party activity it is necessary to carry out everywhere the following measure: at least one-third of the actual party members in the centers must be permanently forbidden to act as party members and Soviet officials at the same time.

The forth basic demand of the Workers' Opposition is this: the party must reverse its policy to the elective principle.

Appointments must be permissible only as exceptions, but lately they began to prevail as a rule. Appointments are very characteristic of bureaucracy, and yet at present they are a general, legalized and well-recognized daily occurrence. The procedure of appointments produces a very unhealthy atmosphere in the party, and disrupts the relationship of equality among the members by rewarding friends and punishing enemies as well as by other no less harmful practices in our party and Soviet life. Appointments lessen the sense of duty and responsibility to the masses in the ranks of appointees, for they are not responsible to the masses. This condition makes the line of division between the leaders and the rank and file members still sharper.

Every appointee, as a matter of fact, is beyond any control, for the leaders are not able to watch closely his activity while the masses cannot call him to account and discharge him if necessary. As a rule every appointee is surrounded by an atmosphere of officialdom, servility and blind subordination, which infects all subordinates, and discredits the party. The practice of appointments rejects completely the principle of collective work; it breeds irresponsibility. Appointments by the leaders must be done away with, and replaced by the elective principle all along the party line. Candidates shall be eligible to occupy responsible administrative positions only when they have been elected by conferences and congresses.

Finally, in order to eliminate bureaucracy and make the party more healthy, it is necessary to revert to that state of things where all the cardinal questions of party activity and Soviet policy are submitted to the consideration of the rank and file and only after that are supervised by the leaders. This was the state of things when the party was forced to carry on its work in secret—even as late as the time of signing the treaty of Brest-Litovsk.

At present the state of things is altogether different. In spite of the widely circulated promises made by the All-Russian party conference held in September, no less important question than that of concessions was decided for the masses quite unexpectedly. And only due to the sharp controversy that arose within the party centers themselves was the question dealing with the trade unions brought out into the open to be thrashed out in debates.

Wide publicity, freedom of opinion and discussion, right to criticize within the party and among the members of the trade unions—such is the decisive step that can put an end to the prevailing system of bureaucracy. Freedom of criticism, right of different factions to freely present their views at party meetings, freedom of discussion—are no longer the demands of the Workers' Opposition alone. Under the growing pressure from the masses a whole series of measures that were demanded by the rank and file long before the All-Russian conference was held, are recognized and promulgated officially at present. If one only reads the proposals of the Moscow Committee in regard to the party structure he becomes proud of the great influence that is being exerted on the party centers. If it were not for the Workers' Opposition the Moscow Committee would never have taken such a sharp "turn to the left." However, we must not overestimate this "leftism," for it is only a declaration of principles to the congress. It may happen, as it has happened many a time with the decisions of our party leaders during these years, that this radical declaration will be forgotten, for as a rule they are accepted by our party centers only just as the mass impetus is felt, and as soon as life again swings into normal channels the decisions are forgotten.

Did not this happen to the decision of the 8th Congress, whereby it resolved to free the party of all elements who joined it for some selfish motives, and to use discretion in accepting non-working elements? What has become of the decision taken by the party conference in 1920, when it was decided to replace the practice of appointments by recommendations? The inequality in the party still exists in spite of the repeated resolutions passed on this subject. As far as the persecutions inflicted on those comrades who dare to disagree with the decrees from the above are concerned they are still being continued. There are many such instances. If these decisions are not enforced then it is necessary to eliminate the basic cause that interferes with their enforcement, that is, to remove from the party those who are afraid of publicity, strict accountability before the rank and file, and freedom of criticism.

Non-working members of the party, and those workers who fell under their influence, are afraid of all this. It is not enough to clean the party of all non-proletarian elements by registration, to increase the control in time of enrollment, etc., for it is also necessary to create opportunities for the workers to join the party; it is necessary to simplify the admission of workers to the party, to create a more friendly atmosphere in the party itself, so that the workers might feel themselves at home, that in the responsible party officials they see not superiors but more experienced comrades, who are ready to share with them their knowledge, experience and skill, and consider seriously workers' needs and interests. How many comrades, particularly young workers, are driven away from the party just because we manifest our impatience with them by our assumed superiority and strictness, instead of teaching them, bringing them up in the spirit of communism.

Besides the spirit of bureaucracy, an atmosphere of officialdom finds a fertile ground in our party. If there is any comradeship in our party it exists only among the rank and file members.

The task of the party congress is to take into account this unpleasant reality, and ponder over the question: why the Workers' Opposition insists on introducing equality, on eliminating all privileges in the party, and placing under a more strict responsibility to the masses, those administrative officials who are elected by them.

Thus, in its struggle for establishing democracy in the party, and the elimination of all bureaucracy, the Workers' Opposition advances three cardinal principles:

(1) Return to the principle of election all along the line with elimination of bureaucracy, by making all responsible officials answerable to the masses.

(2) Introduction of wide publicity within the party both concerning general questions, and where individuals are involved; paying more attention to the voice of the rank and file (wide discussion of all questions by the rank and file, and their summarizing by the leaders; admission of any member to the meetings of party centers, save when problems discussed require particular secrecy); establishment of freedom of opinion and expression (giving the right not only to criticize freely during discussions, but to use funds for publication of literature proposed by different party factions).

(3) Making the party more of a workers' party with limitations imposed on those who fill offices both in the party and the Soviet institutions at the same time.

This last demand is particularly important and essential for the reason that our party must not only build communism, but prepare and educate the masses for a prolonged period of struggle against world capitalism, which may take on unexpected and new forms. It would be too childish to imagine that having repelled the invasion of the white guard and imperialism on the military fronts, we are free from the danger of a new attack from the world capital which is striving to seize Soviet Russia by roundabout ways; to penetrate into our life, and use the Soviet republic for its own ends. This is the potent danger that we must stand guard against, and herein lies the problem for our party — how to meet the enemy well prepared, how to rally all the proletarian forces around the clear-cut class problems (the other groups of the population will always gravitate to capitalism). To carry on preparations for this new page of our revolutionary history is the duty of our leaders.

The most correct solution of the question will be possible only when we succeed in uniting the party all along the line, not only together with the Soviet institutions, but with the trade unions as well. In the latter case the filling up of offices in both the party and in the trade unions does not only tend to deviate the party policy from the clear-cut class line, but, on the contrary, renders the party more immune to the influences of world capitalism during this coming epoch; influences that are exerted through concessions and trade agreements. To make the Central Committee one of workers is to create such a central committee wherein representatives of the lower layers connected with the masses would not stop to play the role of "parading generals" or a merchant's wedding party and become closely bound with the wide non-partisan working masses in the trade unions, being enabled thereby to formulate the slogans of the time, to express workers' needs, their aspirations, and direct the policy of the party along the class line. Such is the line of the Workers' Opposition. Such is its historic task. And whatever derisive remarks the leaders of our party may employ in order to drive away the Opposition, it is the only vital active force with which it is compelled to contend, and to which it will have to pay attention.

Historical Necessity Of The Opposition

Now it remains to answer: Is the Opposition necessary? Is it necessary on behalf of the world workers' liberation from the yoke of capital to welcome its formation, or is it an undesirable movement, detrimental to the fighting energy of the party, and destructive to its ranks?

Every comrade not prejudiced against the Opposition, and who therefore wants to approach the question with an open mind, and analyze it, not in accordance with what the recognized authorities tell him, will see even from these brief outlines that the Opposition is useful and necessary. It is useful primarily because it has awakened slumbering thought. During these years of the revolution we have been so preoccupied with our pressing affairs that we had ceased to appraise our actions from the standpoint of principle and theory. We have been forgetting that the proletariat can commit grave mistakes not only during the period of struggle for political control, and turn toward the morass of opportunism—but that even during the epoch of the dictatorship of the proletariat such mistakes are possible, particularly when on all sides we are surrounded with stormy waves of imperialism, and when the Soviet republic is compelled to act in the capitalist environment. At such times our leaders must be not only wise "statesman-like" politicians, but also be able to lead the party and the whole working class along the line of class reconcilability and class creativeness, and prepare it for a prolonged struggle against the new forms of seizure of the Soviet republic by bourgeois influences of world capitalism. "Be ready, be clear—but along the class lines"—such must be the slogan of our party now more than ever.

The Workers' Opposition has put these questions into the order of the day, rendering thereby its historical service. The thought begins to move, members began to analyze what has already been done, and wherever there is criticism, analysis, where thought moves and works, there is life, progress, advancement forward toward the future. There is nothing more frightful and harmful than sterility of thought and standards of routine. We have been retiring into routine, and might inadvertently have gone off the direct class road leading to communism, if it were not for the Workers' Opposition injecting itself into the situation at a time when our enemies were about to burst into joyful laughter. At present this is already impossible. The Congress and, therefore, the party will be compelled to contend with the point of view expressed by the Workers' Opposition, and either to compromise or make essential concessions under its influence and pressure.

The second service of the Workers' Opposition is that it has brought up for discussion the question as to who, after all, shall be called upon to create new forms of economy, whether it shall be the technicians, men of affairs who by their psychology are bound-up with the past, and Soviet officials with communists scattered among them, or the working class collectives which are represented by the unions?

The Workers' Opposition has said what has long ago been printed in "The Communist Manifesto" by Marx and Engels, viz.: "Creation of communism can and will be the work of the toiling masses themselves. Creation of communism belongs to workers."

Finally, the Workers' Opposition has raised its voice against bureaucracy, and has dared to say that bureaucracy binds the wings of self-activity and the creativeness of the working class; that it deadens thought, hinders initiative and experimenting in the sphere of finding new approaches to production, in a word — it hinders development of new forms for production and life.

Instead of a system of bureaucracy it proposes a system of self-activity for the masses. In this respect the party leaders even now are making concessions and "recognizing" the deviations as being harmful to communism and detrimental to the working class interests (the rejection of centralism). The Tenth Congress, we understand, will make another series of concessions to the Workers' Opposition. Thus, in spite of the fact that the Workers' Opposition appeared just as a mere group inside the party only a few months ago, it has already fulfilled its mission, and has compelled the directing party centers to listen to the Workers' sound advice. At present, whatever might be the wrath toward the Workers' Opposition, it has the historical future to support it.

Just because we believe in the vital forces of our party we know that after some hesitation, resistance and circuitous political moves our party ultimately will again follow that path which has been blazed by the elemental forces of the class organized proletarian. There will be no split. If some of the groups shall leave the party they will not be the ones that make up the Workers' Opposition. Only those will fall out who attempt to evolve into principles our temporary deviations from the spirit of the Communist program, which were forced upon the party by the prolonged civil war, and will hold to them as if they were the essence of our political line of action.

All that part of the party which has been accustomed to reflect the class point of view of the ever growing giant-proletariat will absorb and digest everything that is wholesome, practical and sound in the Workers' Opposition. Not in vain will the rank and file worker speak with assurance and reconciliation: "Ilyich (Lenin) will ponder, think over, listen to us, and then will decide to turn the party rudder toward the Opposition. Ilyich will be with us yet."

The sooner the party leaders will take into account the Oppositions' work, and follow the road marked by the rank and file members, the quicker we shall pass through the crisis in the party at such a difficult time, and the sooner we shall step over the destined line beyond which humanity, having freed itself from the objective economic laws and, profiting by the rich scientific treasure of the workers' collective, will consciously begin to create the human history of the Communist epoch.